Transcendence

The Evolution of Love & Relationships

by Bryan Wesley

About Me

My name is Bryan Omar Wesley and I reside in Huntsville, Alabama. I graduated from Johnson High School in the year 2007 and started writing poetry earlier than that, at the ripe age of 14. It started as a hobby then evolved as a passion. For many years I wrote poems, some to ladies who liked and admired, while other poems were on various topics, as life went on and my experiences started to grow. I started getting into a wide range of relationships as I got older which triggered me to venture off into entering poetry contests and writing for the sheer love of poetry. In my prior works of poetry, I spoke on love, depression, sex, heartbreak and much more. I took a brief hiatus from poetry after a breakup but regained my composure and got back to work and significantly improved on my craft. As I reached my 20's, I began to perform my poetry at open mic nights. With my passion for poetry growing day by day, I decided to share my poetry with the world so they, too, can be introduced to the author, Bryan Wesley.

About The Book

Transcendence is a book series that will explore the depths of love, dating, relationships, games and everything that surrounds it. Unfortunately, it seems like relationships nowadays have taken a turn for the worst. Are we taking steps backwards? Or is this a change towards the future? Are we out for our own desires and needs or is all this just part of the game when dealing with men and women.

In this book and future installments, I will show you how to handle situations and circumstances that will arise as well as advice and tips to help you in the long run and to prepare you for what's to come. The best weapon in your arsenal is preparation; don't lose your morals, dignity or instincts. And most importantly, don't lose yourself.

Acknowledgments

- Bryant Marbury(Dad)
- Deann Marbury(Mom)
- Marquez Marbury
- Latesha Bright
- Kelly Gibbs
- Ashley Charest
- Shikiena Asberry
- Breanna Burt
- Jessica Toney
- Diondra Turner
- Joanna Robinson
- Ebony Ford (editor)
- Shanika Zeiger
- Jalissa Mickle
- Sharon Rice
- Patrice Greer
- Danetria Rice
- John Langford
- Victoria Bell
- Sherika Gaines
- Mrs. Oliver

Thank you all for your kind words, wisdom, and motivation. Without you all this book wouldn't be possible. THANK YOU I LOVE EACH & EVERY ONE OF YOU.

Table of Contents

Chapter 1: The Inauguration

Since the dawn of time, men and women have evolved and matured beyond possibilities, especially when it comes to dating, love, relationships, sex, games and manipulation. Even the way we date has definitely changed; courtship and its' art has been through many transformations. Believe it or not, there are some places that arrange marriages, not for love, but economic stability and other reasons. Can you imagine your family planning and staging a wedding for you and a stranger? This new generation of serial daters and millennials would flip out and cause chaos. Nowadays dating varies from country to country and changes often and with the way men/women run game, manipulate and practice other such tactics for personal gain, both sexes to put up a wall around their heart so they won't fall victim to these practices. Fifty to sixty years ago when dating was commonly referred to as courting, couples tended to date one person at a time; there wasn't many "friends-with-benefits" or anything of that nature going on. Couples attended matinee to checkout new releases on movies, they took walks in the park or would drive around just checking out the scenery of the town. They spent the evening visiting relatives here and there and simply enjoyed time with one another. In regards to teenagers of that time period, there wasn't any staying out late or spending the night. If you didn't pay bills you didn't have that privilege. Parents during this time would often say "Get a house of your own if you want to be grown." Parental influence weighed more back in those days, especially when came to dating. If your folks didn't like the person you were courting it typically ended right there but even back then you had individuals who acted on their own merit. The methods to their own method included rebellion, social status, exploration of their own identity and many other characteristics. Dating isn't hard; it's just a matter of being yourself and finding a person who is best suitable for you but with that can come stress because of womanizers, players, pimps. People are guarding there hearts more nowadays; I mean after all, heartbreak is one of the most painful things to experience. Both sexes have been getting their heartbroken since the beginning of time but one thing both males and females have in common is that neither wants to be lied to or hurt in such a way that they never want to enjoy and experience the essence of love and all that it has to offer. Love has the power to shift moods, ease stress in many forms and turn your dark cloudy day into a blissful joy full of smiles. To some, love is strength but can be a weakness, especially for hopeless romantics of both genders. As the world is shifting and changing around us, some things change and others remain the same. Dating is a beautiful thing and can be fun for men and women. Dating started out as a fair and fun activity for opposite sexes who were interested in each other; there wasn't many games or complications or any of that nonsense. Now granted, it still was trifling and deceitful things going on but a lot of men/women were generally honest with their intentions whether they wanted a relationship or just sex. Because of the values and morals of how some people were raised, not many people tolerated any type of foolishness and both genders generally had good communication by expressing their desires, feelings, emotions to each other. Men were gentlemen with enough confidence lead a country and women were ladies with tons of style and grace. It was an era truly marked with class, status and values. But as time went on, things changed with the rise of single parent homes, male/female roles shifting, society, technology, etc. It has lead us to where we are now. Dating is in a state of disequilibrium and imbalance where some factors don't matters and some outweigh others. When it comes to love, the alter is like a battlefield with men versus women. Dating feels more like a warzone with opposing sides coming up with a strategy or trying to gain an advantage and win but in the battle, both sides may win temporarily, but in the long term, both sides are losing, because we are only hurting ourselves. We'll never find the right person with the right mentality that some men/women nowadays have. A lot of people drop their standards and morals beyond belief. More men and women have trust issues, marriages are falling apart, people commit infidelity, but it's not all crazy and chaotic. Some are still positive in the world and it is great men and women out here but we're just caught in a world where people seem to be overly materialistic, full of "swag", have low self-value, low standards, etc. All of this and more has contributed to how the dating and relationships are now. Men nowadays tend to act more like boys and instead of leading by example they following as if this was twitter instead of stepping up to the plate as men about the situation. They've gotten used to running from not handling responsibilities as a man. For women as well they are lowering their standards and values, flashing their bodies on social networks for likes and attention and being little girls instead of grown women. The future of dating and relationships is bright because as we get older, the boys and girls start to separate themselves from the men and women; some of us start to make better relationship decisions and start to look for more long term stability in our companion. Dating can definitely be a roller coaster at times but it is also based on how you approach it and your mindset as an individual. If you have your head on right, approach the dating game from an honest and mature standpoint.

This Thing Called Love

Besides money the thing we often praise,

Will have crying for days,

Have us in a daze,

Or questioning & changing our ways

It is the very thing that could end in disaster

Or have you living happy ever after

Tisk tisk

This thing is a major risk,

It can break your heart or put you in romantic bliss

This thing we want & crave

Can last an eternity or fade

An unbreakable bond between two

Wedding vows & saying 'I do'

This thing comes with great expectation

Give you butterflies & warm sensation

Takes effort & patience, to build maturation

On the path to a great relation

It can be a fairytale turned to a dream

Love it's the most beautiful thing

Words of Wisdom

- Ladies if he ignore your calls during the day then he doesn't deserve to see you at night.
- Fellas if she doesn't accept you at your worst then she doesn't deserve you at your best
- Men & Women relationships should flow like this: Talking-→ Dating→ Relationships. But there is an exception to every rule.
- If you were happy before someone came into your life, you can be happy after they leave.
- Protect your heart; don't give it away until somebody has proven themselves worthy.
- A relationship is an addition not a completion.
- What separates a woman from a girl is her priorities.
- A real man is dedicated to one woman and not a bunch of hoes.
- Time heals a broken heart; not jumping from relationship to relationship.
- The best relationships start as friendships
- Seek a relationship with someone you can build with not just someone to be with.
- You must love yourself before you go searching for a relationship.
- If he/she is bringing you more stress & tears then love & happiness then they don't deserve you.
- Nobody can define you only you can define yourself.

Chapter 2: Kickin' It Old School

Back in the day men and women dated a certain way they didn't play too many games or tricks but these methods did exist between both sides. In the south, dating was commonly referred to as coating (courting); this is when two people are interested in dating each other. People during this time dated with a sense of enthusiasm and purpose. They hung out a lot and generally went to movies/matinee; if they had cars, some would drive around for hours at a time either getting food, hanging out with friends and family or discussing daily life, stress and a future together. Now during this time you just couldn't bring anybody to see your parents. Why? Well, because people during this time teens and young adults' dating habits was heavily influenced by their parents. If mom and dad didn't like your potential boyfriend/girlfriend, then it was case closed because a parent's word was often considered law back then. They didn't allow their children to spend the night with the opposite sex or any of that nonsense. Most parent's views were: "If you want to spend the night, get your own place and start paying bills." There was not many single parent homes back then because, generally, couples stuck together through the rollercoaster ride of life and honored those sacred vows of 'til death do us part.' In some cases, they stayed together for the kids and instilled knowledge, wisdom and responsibilities into them to help them with the journey of life. But we all know that at times, life itself can be our best teacher. Dating and relationships can be a tough course to master but back in the day, the concept of dating was simple. Be with the one who makes you the most happiest and complete as a person. Men and women generally dated one at a time; there was not any friends with benefits going on. Men and women just picked one person and went from there; they were very open and wore their hearts on their sleeves. Vulnerability was definitely a possibility but high risk equals high rewards for both sexes. Society's view of relationships during this time was strict but a lot of men and women dated at their own pace and remained true to their standards/morals; these standards built the bridge for the relationships. Men carried themselves with confidence and were providers as well as protectors and they had to convey this during the dating process also remain true to themselves. Men during this time were attracted to the women with pretty eyes and large breasts; this type of lady was very sought out, sometimes even more then with ladies with personalities. A typical 'guy approach' during this time was simple and straight forward. They didn't beat around the bush or let the opportunity pass them by. Some might have been a little intimidated but the majority was fearless and went head first to the apple of their eye. They approached, then laid down their intentions and if the lady was interested she either went with his advances and either they dated or she rejected him and he moved on. Women during this time were gracious and flirty in subtle manner and had respect for themselves as ladies. They upheld their standards and if you couldn't meet them then it was your loss. If you could meet their standards and expectations, then you had a chance. It was just a matter of keeping up and growing together as potential couple and as individuals too. Women of this time were interested in a tall masculine man with a strong build; this viewpoint was seen as essential because it was slightly protective and macho. Ladies during this time dated but it came with restrictions from parents and if they were young adults they maintained self-control plus they always knew when to exit gracefully exactly the same way they entered the scene. There wasn't too much casual dating. Ladies of this time wanted boyfriends rather than husbands and they knew how to separate the men from the boys. They quickly cut the boys as if this was tryouts for a basketball team. Men were the pursuers and the ladies were the object of their affection. A woman's first love of their life is their dad; every man gets compared to the almighty dad in their life. He sets the bar and the potential suitors try to match it in every way possible. This is also the case with men too because they valued qualities that a woman possessed similar to their own mother. As a guy, one thing is for certain, you just couldn't disrespect a lady of this era. They knew their worth and would gladly leave you without a thought or hesitation. Sex wasn't something that was planned; couples went with the flow of their relationship. Men and women of this time worked out any potential issues and if they didn't, they went their separate ways. Dating during this time period wasn't too stressful but, of course you had the players, pimps and "femme fatals" of their time but character flaws were easy to see. Only to the untrained eye, can the 'bad apples' of the bunch have any success with it. It was a fun time to date and have a relationship; both sexes pretty much bring their A game, the men got separated from the boys and the ladies got separated from the childish little girls of the bunch. Men/women had a way of dating that we now view as 'old school' but having an old school mindset isn't based on words it's having genuine intentions to treat a person well and to have a great, fun time as well. Dating the 'old school' way has to flow thru your blood stream and live in the most precious place.........The Soul.

Everlasting Love

3:01pm was the time,

You crossed my path & took over my mind,

Both of us being a Leo sign,

We dated then fell in love,

Sweet addiction love was our drug,

We kiss, we fuss, we fight,

We argue then we make love all night,

Thru the cries, laughs, & fears,

We made it thru the years,

I captured your heart,

Said vows till death do us part,

Thru sickness & health,

True love takes two,

When I die I'm getting buried next to you,

So much love passion,

Our love is everlasting.

Words of Wisdom

- Fellas, don't push away the only loyal lady who supports you. Instead, open up to her and express how you feel; it's no need to worry if she's riding with you until the wheels fall off.
- Nobody wants to be with someone who is always pointing out the bad in them and never acknowledging the good.
- Women desire affection, comfort, communication, honestly, love, security and happiness.
- Ladies stop crying over him; instead use that strength to get over him.
- Ladies, a real man won't disrespect what you stand for.
- Every relationship you've had is a reflection of your choices and decisions. If you want a different result, make a different choices.
- Being in a relationship is a full time job, so don't apply if you're not ready to put in work.
- Ladies, sometimes the best guys for you are the ones you're ignoring and pushing away.
- She'd rather be independent and be her own team of me, myself and I then be on your team of hoes. She is a woman who holds her own.
- Fellas, the right lady will bring out the best in you. The wrong kind will bring out the stress and headaches.
- Silence is a lady's loudest cry. You can always tell she's really hurt when she starts ignoring you.
- One of the toughest decisions you'll have to face is to either walk away or try harder.

Chapter 3: Modern Technology

One thing that has vastly effected dating and relationships over the past years has been technology. It has affected the dating game in so many ways and in some cases, has improved it to a certain extent. We, as men and women, have adapted to these advances in technology and used them to our benefit and advantages. Using technology at your disposal can give you a big leverage with the opposite sex or can give you the upper hand over the competition in your own gender. In the right hands, it can be used as communication, charm, wit, support, etc. but in the wrong hands it can be used as manipulation, deception and bad intentions but it all depends on the individual. Men, often used to being the pursuers, tend to use technology as a means of contact, persuasion, and initializing an interaction with a lady. If used right, and in an effective manner, this can raise a lady's attraction and/or interest level. Failure to use technology the right way can push the right lady in the wrong direction; it can be used as a means of flirting or creating interest but on the opposite end, a lady can come off as clingy or crazy if technology isn't used correctly. Back in the day when a man and woman were interested in each other, they either exchanged home numbers or the guy got the lady home number, during this period of time there weren't any cell phones, just house phones. You call a lady, and most likely a relative or younger sibling would pick up and right then is where a guy would say "Yes, is so-and-so home?" If so, then the man and woman would talk on the phone for minutes, sometimes, hours but this often depended on how many siblings he/she had because they might want to use the phone too. Some parents set certain times where they didn't allow phone calls. Now, as time went on, technology went forward and soon came beepers. This added a new element to the game it expanded communication between men and women; but on the downside, it gave men/women access to whoever they were dating/talking to. Having that much access means you can keep up with their whereabouts and see what they are doing. Soon, as time moved forward and beepers phased out, then came cell phones. This new addition to the dating game changed the landscape as we know it and then texting became a part, as well. But in some ways it was bad. It provided instant messaging but conversation and communication has slacked off, and has pretty much being replaced. People these days rather text then talk on the phone; a 10 minute conversation nowadays has been replaced by 10-15 replies on a cell phone between two people. Conversations range from bland to generic to exciting based on the individual. In recent years, certain strategic measures have become a part of texting and communication in general. A lot of men and women have now implemented a technique known as "curving" or simply "swerve." This is when someone ignores you or ignores what you're saying and it's pretty much done on purpose. Some men and women like to address things on their own time and basis when they are ready, while others may not address the subject or matter at all for their own benefit. The art of curving is mainly done during texting but can be used in other forms. Every individual texts in their own special unique way and expresses him/herself in an expressive way. The use of texting lingo and emoji can shift the emotion and feel of a text conversation. The most common emoji is a smiley face that is used to convey happiness. The most flirtatious emoji is the wink face, and some people use these emoji's unconsciously at times but most know what they are doing. Technology in the modern age has progressed greatly with online dating. A percentage of today's relationships began online and the internet provides many advantages and disadvantages to dating. It's convenient, fun, straight to the point and can be satisfying but on the other end, it can be misleading, dangerous, time consuming and very frustrating. When it comes to online dating with both sexes, men tend to lie about such things as age, height and income, whereas women lie most about weight, physical build and age. One other major recent phenomenon in online dating is called "catfished." The term means someone who pretends to be someone they're not using social media to create false identities and to pursue deceptive online romance. But nonetheless, this hasn't stopped some from using online romance as an option in the dating game. Social networking sites such as Facebook, Twitter, Instagram, etc. are also major factors in the dating game. With social networking sites, you can keep up with crushes, old friends, exes or cyberstalk the object of your desire on a daily basis. This opens up many opportunities for dating and communication and, of course, flirting. With a site such as Instagram, you can simply tap a photo or use the recently added feature known as being able to Instagram direct an individual at free will. This presents an opportunity to share private photos with somebody or if you are bold, you comment on their photos with your intentions like "Hey baby, hit me up" or to attract their attention by taping each one of their photos. This method draws attention to you by blowing up their notifications so that the next time they log on, they will see you. With Twitter, you can DM (Direct Message) your object of desire but, as a reminder, this comes with a 142 character limit so you have to choose your words precisely and correctly. The other tools you have in your arsenal are being able to favorite their tweets or retweet the object of your desire. You can also test your boldness and initiate a casual conversation with them and see where that takes you. Now with Facebook, you can inbox your object of desire followed by "liking" or "sharing" tons of their statuses but a large percentage of everything happens in the inbox. But tread carefully; there is a difference between persistence and annoyance. Modern technology is forever changing and shifting each day with a multitude of options at your disposal. You can pick up your IPad and search for singles on E-harmony website or log on to a social networking site and try your luck there but whatever route you choose to take be yourself first and foremost.

Past Meets Future

Our youth was a joy,
As youngsters we played tag & Gameboy,
I shared my Oreos, you shared your chips ahoy,
We watched TV & played in the sandbox,
Had water balloon fights & threw rocks
Having fun from sun up til sun down
We stayed playing around,
But it was one faithful day,
You packed up & moved away,
I was left all alone,
Playing with toys all on my own,
A true friend is what I lacked,
No matter the tears you wasn't coming back,
I grew up at my own pace,
I discovered your profile on Myspace,
I had searched for you relentlessly,
I wrote you then you responded instantly,
Look at you fully grown,
I soon saved your number in my smartphone,
We met up for the first time in years,
Past meets future as it appears,
Our time was full of joy & cheers
We laughed & reminisce,
Being reunited was my ultimate wish,
Having you in my life I felt just fine,
Now let's make up for last time.

Words of Wisdom

- If you were happy before you met someone, you can be happy after they're gone.
- This generation of men/women is so stubborn; two people will think about each other all day but won't text or call each other.
- Ladies, if the only time he comes over is for sex then you know where you stand with him.
- If he doesn't answer or return your texts during the day, then he doesn't deserve to see you late at night.
- Don't confuse still being in love, when you're just attached to what's familiar.
- There is a difference between what we look for, what we settle for, and what we are meant for.
- No girl wants to be with a guy that can't let other girls know he taken.
- Ladies, stop messing with seasonal dudes, they are not built for the long term.
- Don't let lust confuse you and have you make crazy mistakes.
- Never allow people's opinions to shape your relationships.
- Actions prove who someone is words just prove who they want to be.
- Separate your needs and wants before you go searching for a relationship.
- Little girls chase after looks and swag but mature ladies fall for loyalty, respect, proper treatment and security.
- Don't go chasing a relationship if you don't have yourself together yet.
- Don't run back to previous pain and hurt. Take that time to work on yourself and find love for yourself.

Chapter 4: Modern Man

The men of this generation are very different from their predecessors. This is because of many factors such as environment, experiences, technology and so forth. Each individual man is different in their own way with their own personalities; as boys grow they soon shift into men, some quicker than others. The lessons of life will hit a man early in life or hit him late but it will hit him. Many boys are shaped by role models and father figures early but some modern men were taught a certain psyche, either by instilled strong masculinity or athletes of feminine characteristics. Being raised in such a household can be a gift and a curse to the modern man. On one hand, he is getting parental guidance and motherly love, but on the other hand, as the saying goes: It often takes a man to raise one. But remember, there is an exception to every rule. As the modern man reaches his teens, his values and morals start to form and he is now on his way to becoming a man but there is just one problem: everything he has been taught and brought up on now conflicts with new trials and peer pressure of life. The modern man now has to make a decision; does he use the knowledge and teachings he was taught by his single mother or does he live and learn by taking risks and trying something new? Many youthful experiences can shape a boy into a man; it could be his first rejection or first heartbreak or maybe even his first relationship. Whatever the experience is, a lot of boys during this stage start to figure out what works and what doesn't. A lot of "overly-masculine" boys will start to notice a trend that includes being considered a 'bad boy' or 'jerk' that may potentially give them better success with girls. This may find them going through a string of little girlfriends here and there. Based on the results, a boy may continue with what works for them or they may adapt and change their ways as time goes on. Now the other boys who may have a tiny bit of femine ways and can relate to women may not have been pursued as much as the more masculine boys. Guys of this nature may have been seen as 'just friends' or 'not their type' or maybe even ignored altogether. These types of boys seemed to lack a certain appeal to girls; although some could say this is all based on immaturity of young minds but this trend continues for some as they age. With age and progression comes, also, choices and consequences. Do you do what's right for yourself or what's right for the situation and circumstances? The answer to such a question is based on your mentality. There are two types of fella's: boys and men. Some would argue that they are both the same but that's is not correct at all. The difference between a man and a boy is how they handle pivotal moments and situations. Boys follow while men lead by example. A boy will make a thousand excuses while a man will make one promise and rise to the occasion like the king he rightfully is. A boy can progress to a man but a man is the ultimate pinnacle of excellence. Both may make mistakes but a man learns from his mistakes and looks to improve upon them. Many women will make the mistake of dating a boy but once they date a man there isn't any turning back because a real man is a provider, protector, and leader and is also loyal to only one woman. But a boy is one who isn't ready, a follower, one who likes to play games and rather have quantity over quality. A real man knows that the castle has only one valuable treasure and that treasure is its' queen. With the modern man, the vast majority will sometimes play to their advantage while other man does what is considered right, which can be considered a matter of opinion. The men who play to their advantage are only doing what works for them whether it is wrong or right; they don't care. It's all about them and this is selfishness at its best. Some modern men don't date as much as guys from previous generations, instead they rather ask a lady to "come and chill" or they may ask a chick to come over and "vibe" with them. That may involve a movie, smoking, drinking, etc. and the reason a lot of modern man don't date as much is because some feel they don't have to wine and dine a lady. They know that if the attraction is mutual on both ends, they won't have to put in as much work. Granted, some of these guys are just lazy and lack work ethic while others know that they don't have to necessarily date certain woman with a low self-worth. A simple "come by and chill" will do the trick but, remember, this all based on the type of woman he is dealing with. This just an example of a few men, not all of them. The few that do "come over and chill" aren't looking for a serious long term relationship or commitment; some are only looking for a little thrill, fun, and just casual sex, not anything serious. And if they can't get what they want from that lady (which is usually sex), they won't care because the modern man lives by the saying "don't chase them, just replace them." The vast majority of modern men can be described as careless, unemotional, hard exterior, selfish, cocky demeanor and rebel soul but this is just a percentage of all guys. Some modern men are absolute gentlemen and have great hearts but they just need an opportunity. Another percentage of modern men man grew up very fast and in rough circumstances. They had to "tough up" very fast as they grow and mature. These will either evolve into bad boys, gentlemen, skimps, mama boys, etc. but it all depend on their experiences. The best way to deal with and handle the modern man is to not control him or try to change him. Instead, try setting standards about yourself as a woman; this will go a long way for you in the long run. Because if a man wants to be with you, he will adapt and better himself as a person and either reach your standards or surpass them. It all depends on what type of man he is. The future of the modern man all depends on him. He has to make a choice and be ready for the possible consequences. The modern man has so many abilities; he can be nothing or he can be the boyfriend type or a loving husband. The future is bright it all depends on the man himself.

Boy vs Gentleman

A boy will lie & look to gain,
A boy will cause you a lot of pain,
His excuses will drive you insane,
He lacks loyalty and trust
A boy only understands lust,
A boy is quick to react,
His words & actions never match,
He states fiction instead of fact,
A boy follows but never leads,
That's why he fails and never succeeds,
A Gentleman will rise to the occasion,
Gives you a tingling sensation,
Give euphoria & feelings of jubilation
He'll make love to you with passion
His words are backed up with action
He'll hold your hand & kiss your cheek
Massage ya body & caresses ya feet
Give you respect
Make love til sunset,
A boy is a pretender while a man is a contender,
A gentleman will place a ring on ya finger.

Words Of Wisdom

- Fellas, never neglect your lady. You may think the grass is greener on the other side but it's greater where you water it.
- Fellas, don't chase what's between a woman's legs. Go after the most important: Her heart.
- Boys make excuses, Men take action.
- Having a real woman by your side is a true blessing so fellas, be thankful and cherish the fact that a woman of that nature chose you.
- A real man takes care of his kids.
- Fellas, if she rejects you, just move on. There's no need to disrespect her or call her out of her name.
- Fellas, be loyal and faithful to one lady.
- A real man shows with his actions rather than saying with his words.
- Fellas, don't down your lady. Bring her up.
- Fellas, work ethic and consistency will take you a long way to achieving your goals.
- Be a man of your word.
- Fellas, a lady doesn't want to just drink and smoke with you. Take her out on a date or try something spontaneous.
- Fellas, respect a lady like you want a guy to respect your mother, sister, aunt or cousin.
- Fellas, it's not how many times you get knocked down but how many times you rise up.
- Always understand the castle is only big enough for one king and one queen
- Fellas always maintain your standards and values.
- Don't be a so called "Real Nigga;" be a real man.

Chapter 5: Modern Woman

The modern woman is a type that has been through many experiences in her youth from heartbreak to lies, disappointment, physical abuse and much more. The modern woman had to grow fast in life; some modern women are a product of their environment and simply need to venture off into new scenery but that is up to that particular woman to make that decision on her life. The modern woman grew up, typically, in a household with both parents available or, for a large majority, she may have grew up in a single parent home with there being a strong possibility of no father figure in the house. The ladies who grew up with a strong father or male presence typically made better relationship decisions versus women without positive male presence around. A lot of the choices for the ladies without dads about men were based off their peers and television or what they thought was popular. It's a bit harder for those types of modern women to date because they don't have an idea of what a man is supposed to be like, what qualities he is to possess or how he is supposed to treat a lady. All they know what to go by is what they see and how they feel but what they feel is often temporary feeling and not meant to last for the long term. The other ladies with a male presence in their life are prone to making mistakes, as well, but as they adjust and adapt, their decision making will get better and soon, their choices will get better as well. As the modern woman grows up, she'll get her first boyfriend then soon after she will experience her first kiss. As a little girl depending on these experiences in her youth, she will grow an understanding of the opposite sex and as she matures both mentally and physically, she will learn to see life in a new perspective. The modern woman either had a very strict mother or a mother that didn't care as much. Some had one in the middle that was balanced out. The modern woman usually did pretty well in school; she balanced her school work and dating perfectly even when stressed. This type of lady handles herself with style and poise. The modern woman doesn't have many female friends for various reasons and she most likely has a bit of tomboy in her. She thinks women are full of drama so she prefers the company of men rather than women. It may even go back to when the modern woman was a little girl; her little bit of tomboyish side and masculinity started to grow. Maybe even having a tough older brother in the house played a part but for this reason, the modern woman prefers the company of guys rather than girls. The modern woman may make mistakes and date a long line of "Mr. Wrongs" but some will adjust and make corrections while others may take a while for them to learn the error of their ways. A select bunch they may never learn. Life is our best teacher and life will make you learn the easy way or the hard way; it all comes down to the lady and the decisions she chooses to make. The modern woman can seem like a lot to handle to the untrained but if a man was to look deep inside with this type of woman, he would see that she is a very precious soul on the inside. The modern woman puts up a tough front because life, in itself, has taught her to show no love because showing love is a sign of weakness and vulnerability. Love is the very thing that has broken their hearts since childhood; love is what has disappointed them time after time. For the modern woman, love is a tough pill to swallow and some don't even have any idea what love is because they never felt it nor received it a day in their lives. They are familiar with lust and infatuation because some modern women are very attracted to the 'glitz and glamour.' They are attracted to the swag of how a guy carries himself and the way a guy talks with a certain confidence mixed with slang. This swag may attract some but not all women are attracted to this type of man nor are they attracted to "swag." Some modern women are more into personality and qualities of a man in general. The reason for the strong attraction to materialism is because for, some modern ladies, they grew up in poor conditions and greed and materialism is a sense power to the ladies. It makes them feel like they are somebody when really deep down in that spirit of theirs, is a small little girl begging for help and is very insecure. The morals and values of modern woman all depends on the individual lady but having both will go a long way for any lady in the long run, especially in the dating game. Modern women's biggest strength in the dating game is sex appeal; having such a powerful weapon can do wonders for a lady. The modern woman doesn't pursue, she merely does the picking and choosing of the suitors. Who she picks can be based on various factors such sexual attraction, class, status, or her mindset at that current moment. Modern woman don't make a decision based on the long term. It's usually based on how she feels at that moment in her life. The same decision she may think is good at age twenty may turn out to be something she regrets at age of twenty-five but as life goes on, experience will be her best teacher as well as an ultimate guide to life. The modern woman is very balanced and adaptable in dating. You can wine and dine her or just chill and relax with her as long as you provide her with respect, great conversation, smiles and fun. She is all yours but understand that this type of lady gets very bored and needs lots of attention because for some modern women, they didn't get a lot of attention from daddy growing up because he was nonexistent. The modern woman at her worst can be like a child: always needing attention, sneaky, manipulative, and vindictive in the worst way but how to understand and handle these types comes down to assessing whether or not you are messing with a girl or a grown woman. The modern woman, at her best, will be mature, independent, loving, a queen and his ingredient to his success. She may be a lot to handle but the modern woman is worth it in every way possible. When you meet the right one she won't just be an addition, she will be the icing on the cake; a big cake that you'll soon give her with your last name and a ring on her finger.

Beautiful Woman

Beautiful complexion & magnificent eyes
Your smile is a sun shine in the skies,
You walk with confidence,
You glow with radiance,
You exhibit exuberance
I admire your independence,
No man is needed,
Your goals you achieve it,
The success ladder you climb
Libra is your sign,
You make your intentions clear,
Haters you don't fear,
Drama you don't entertain,
Success you want to obtain,
You don't tolerate BS,
You always at your best,
Nobody else is on par,
Beautiful woman is what you are.

Words of Wisdom

- Sex is an amazing ingredient to a relationship but it should never be the only reason two people are together.

- Ladies, you shouldn't have to get naked in front of him for him to see your heart. He should love you and treat you as a queen regardless of what you wear.

- Ladies, stop trying to date guys and playing the role of Mrs. Fix It.

- Ladies, any guy can see your tears but it takes someone truly special to understand what they mean.

- Those "I'm sorry baby" and him taking you for granted gets old. If he's giving you more excuses then improvement then cut him loose.
- Time heals a broken heart, not jumping from relationship to relationship.

- Classy ladies fight to defend themselves while ratchet chicks fight because they're bored or miserable with their lives.

- The best thing a woman can wear is her smile.

- Ladies, a relationship is an addition not a completion.

- Girls cling while ladies let go with class and dignity.

- Ladies, don't plan the wedding while he's still planning the first date …. Let things play out.

- Ladies, if you don't trust him, the last thing you should be doing is having sex with him.

Chapter 6: Anatomy of Attraction

One of the biggest factors in dating and how men and women relationships potentially shift forward is sexual attraction. That means seeing or knowing someone and not just desiring them plus finding them attractive but thinking you would like to have sex with them. At its strongest, sexual attraction can cause you to daydream, get butterflies, sweat or simply getting turned on in an uncontrollable way. Now, let's not get confused; there is a small difference between sexual attraction and sexual desire. When it comes to sexual attraction you're thinking and feeling a certain way simultaneously. With sexual desire, you actually may try to follow through with actions and as we all know, actions speak a whole lot louder than words. As relationships progress to a serious level among men and women, the topic of sex starts to become the elephant in the room. Pressure mounts plus adrenaline rush but there is one thing that raises the absolute most and that is sexual tension. That is when two individuals interact or are in close proximity to one another and one or both feel a certain level of sexual desire for each other. They can choose to act on it or let it build or ultimately let it fade away as time passes. In some cases, the attraction can be one sided on all ends for either the man or woman. For instance, a guy/girl can feel instant attraction for someone while that person doesn't feel a single thing. That attraction is one sided and can be summed up as unrequited because no matter how much of a great person you are or the good qualities you possess, you can't force a person to like you or be sexually attracted to you. Attraction, in many forms, can be complex between men and women. Sometimes it simply comes down to having "it" or not. Having that certain "it" factor goes a very long way and can be anything; it could be humor, confidence, swagger, charisma, etc. It could also be a combination of many things that an individual may possess. Having one sided attraction can cause you to overthink, as well as, doubt yourself. Having this can be tough for any man or woman but the best solution to the problem is doing a soul search of yourself and knowing your worth as a person. You have to understand that you deserve more as well as better. By deserving more, you should want to feel loved, appreciated, needed and cherished you should want someone who feels exactly the same as you. As far as deserving better, it simply comes down to finding someone who wants to treat you that way. We, as men/women, all deserve love; take each day one at a time. Attraction is a strong powerful force that we all experience at different parts of our life and as we begin to grow, we adapt to handling it in the best way we can. Some of us will choose to express it openly, to the person we are attracted to, we can downplay till it goes away or we can live in denial with ourselves. One of the biggest factors that can shift attraction is time itself. This is because in time, everything about how we feel can change. It may take one month or five years but things can possibly change. Remember, possibly, every man/woman is different and gets turned on by different things. Change is something we can't foresee or predict accurately, for the most part, but we, as humans, tend to judge a book by its cover too often nowadays. Once we meet a person, we immediately assess in every shape possible. We are looking at their clothes, the way they carry themselves and the way they talk. After we assess them, we then form an opinion of them and go from there. Not everyone does this but majority do. Often times, our attraction can rule over our thoughts and emotions to the point we may let certain things slide that we normally wouldn't. Yes, sadly, attraction can affect judgment. For some, this leads to infatuation which can then lead to heartbreak or disappointment in dating. Sometimes, our own desires lead to us getting hurt because we place high importance on what we want instead of what we need. The very thing that we need, we push away; it's strange that the person we often ignore is the one who adores us but the one we adore is the one who ignores us or mistreats us. Attraction has that effect on us sometimes. Some ladies prefer a challenge or seek a "thrill." Since the beginning of time, women have had a certain lust for excitement, especially when it comes to guys. Some would prefer a man who is spontaneous and unpredictable because you never know what you are going to get. Often times, what you may get might be love or on the other hand it could be pain; all of this is based on the individual you desire. Both men and women find different things and people sexy. What might look good to you might not be attractive to someone else because beauty is in the eye of the beholder. Typically, men like women who are similar to their mothers (quality wise) and as far as physical attributes, some men prefer a lady with a fit body while others may like their lady thick in all the right places. Some fellas' prefer a down-to-earth lady while others may prefer the homeboy-ish type of lady. This is the type of ladies that rather wear sneakers then heels but to each own; the best way to summarize a man taste in women is that men love variety. Ladies taste in men may change in time as they go through many cycles and phases. Many ladies like a masculine man who demonstrates dominance and is a leader; someone who is a protector and a man who knows how to take charge in some ways. As far as physical attributes some prefer a man tall or short with cute features. Some like their man neatly dressed and well groomed because after all presentation is everything.

Attraction is a powerful force like no other but it can be tamed. Always know your worth as a woman/man and never let anybody degrade you or treat you low as dirt. Looks may be deceiving but personality and character go a long way so never lose sight of who you are and what you deserve.

Basic Instinct

An intense attraction like no other
It's no wonder,
I'm dreaming of taking you under,
The sheets,
Taking you to sexual peaks,
Heights unseen, orgasms never felt,
Great sex essential to your health,
Let the sexual tension rise
Let me undress you with my eyes,
You blushing & feeling butterflies,
Let me guide you my way,
On these silk sheets you lay,
Take off your shoes relax your feet,
Breathing heavy as your heart skips a beat,
Rip off your shirt then take off your pants,
Turn around get in a 3 point stance,
Panties ripped, across the room they are flicked
I soon kiss, devour & lick,
Your breasts,
I caress,
I spank you as my child,
Position you in doggy style,
We get freaky & wild,
Soon we climax,
Then relax,
No remorse
Basic instinct & passion took its course

Words of Wisdom

- Gentleman, you can have handsome looks, great personality and be an overall great guy but if there isn't any attraction on her end, there isn't anything you can do except move on.

- Work on improving yourself and the right one will find you.

- Ladies, don't get too emotionally attached off sex.

- Having his baby won't make him stay; he has to want to be with you.

- Don't be someone's down time, spare time, or part time if you're not worth their time.

- Don't complain about something you're putting up with.

- Listen to your heart but know when to trust your mind.

- There comes a time when you have to choose between turning the page or just closing the book.

- Never make permanent decisions based on temporary feelings.

- If he isn't willing to commit to you 100%, then cut off his options.

- You can't control who you're attracted to but you can control whether or not to act on it.

- There is a difference between falling for your type and being a prisoner of your type.

- At the end of the day, it's not about him getting you hot and turned on until you're wet. It's about him showing you respect.

- Having swag may be cute but it will never outmatch personality.

- Lust fades away with time but true love only grows with time.

- The only two things a woman needs is confidence and a smile.

- Good sex doesn't mean anything if it doesn't come from a loyal man/woman.

Chapter 7: Recovery & Rejuvenation

As life goes forward through heartbreak, deception, disappointment and games, one person you must always lookout for the most is yourself. In the world of good and bad, self-preservation is needed and if you fail to do so, you risk greater chances of heartbreak and pain which can take a toll and effect on future relationships with the opposite sex. Heartbreak and pain can cause a person to shut down on all levels; those levels being emotionally, mentally, spiritually. It can cause a person to be bitter, have low confidence and low self-esteem. Some men and women get in a relationship that soon turns sour and maybe eventually fall apart. The end of a sour relationship can result from cheating, unhappiness or the love fading away. No matter the result, some people handle break ups very different and some move forward while others may sulk and be depressed for a while. Some men and women become careless which leads to a path of possible promiscuity. The reason for this is because some individuals hit such a low point in their life that they need to feel loved and wanted. Feeling like this causes people to act out and not be themselves. The road to recovery is often a tough one for both sexes. Contrary to popular belief, men get and feel hurt too on so many levels. The key difference between men and women is that men don't show it as much as women do with heartbreak and pain. When it comes to men, it gets held inside very deep. Sometimes to cope with this, men may exercise or play video games to deal with stress while others may talk to friends or head to the club. As a man you will have rocky and bumpy roads filled with hate and adversity but it's up to the man to uplift himself to see the light at the end of the tunnel and to stay striving until he reaches his ultimate destination. Life can knock you down multiple times but as a man, you have a choice to either lay down or get back up. It all starts with self-evaluation and keeping God first. What doesn't kill you will make you stronger. With ladies, when it comes to heartbreak and pain, they express it more openly. Ladies feel pain more on a deep emotional level so the pain lingers on more and more with some while others deal with their hurt in a different way. Some ladies call up the girls and try to set up a 'girl's night out' for fun and drinks while others turn to close friends or relatives for support. Whatever it takes to feel better, some ladies may try to experiment with casual sex, either with an ex from the past, or a friend but very rarely is this the case for when a woman is down. It will show more in her confidence and her worth as a lady. It's true what they say: have no wrath like a woman scorned. The broken and shattered pieces of a woman heart can be repaired. It all is based on the lady and the steps she takes to move forward with the broken pieces. She can either wait for a man to come and uplift her, which can be a strong a possibility, but never underestimate the strength of a strong woman. A strong woman, with time, will uplift herself. Time is a person's best friend, in some circumstances. That broken heart will be new and repaired as new. All it takes is her knowing her value and worth as a woman and as a person. Past hurt will pave a new way to new experiences, new journeys, new opportunities and, most of all, new blessings. Once a lady says to herself "I am worth it," and decides to take steps to improving her life, the possibilities are endless. In life, we make errors and mistakes from the time as toddlers until the day we are senior citizens. We will forever have learning experiences that shape and mold us. The bad experiences we have are meant to be lessons; no mistake should be made twice but the rollercoaster of life can dish out the unexpected. Life is what you make it; never let one moment or situation change you for the worst. Having a past mistake may be bad but you as an individual can grow and overcome it. It all comes down to the individual.

Rejuvenation

We have our down points in life,
Where we lose sight,
Faith & courage sink,
Tumultuous situations cause us to shrink,
Too much going on don't know what to think,
Nowhere to go,
Feeling low,
But always know,
Blessings is coming soon,
Keep your head high to the moon,
Depression don't last for long,
What don't kill you makes you strong,
Welcome to heavenly bliss,
Sadness now has become happiness,
Cherish & overdose on life,
All that is wrong will soon turn right,
What you thought was a tough situation,
Created tons of growth & rejuvenation.

Words of Wisdom

- Don't count the days, make the days count.

- Stop being afraid of what could go wrong and start focusing on what could go right.

- Success is most achieved by those who don't know that failure is inevitable.

- Stay strong through hard times because hard times don't last long.

- Always remember whoever is trying to bring you down is already below you.

- Every day, choose to focus on the positive in your life.

- Map out your goals; less procrastination and more focus on the destination.

- To start a new chapter on life, you must first close the previous chapter.

- Don't ever be afraid to stand out. Greatness always comes from unique and fearless.

- Sometimes you have to pave your own path to happiness and success.

- Surround yourself with those who improve your life rather than bring you down.

- Master your craft and never let anybody tell you what you can or can't do.

Chapter 8: The Game

One key important thing you got to pay attention to in the dating game is the "game" itself. Game is something men and women both possess and both can use game in a variety of ways to get what they want or to play a situation to their most favorable outcome. Now, what is game? The term has a very broad meaning but I define game as an individual possessing a level of knowledge, abilities, and skills to play a situation in their favor. Having game can be the difference between dating success and dating failure. Those men/women with game tend to enjoy some forms of success while those who lack it may be left to their lonesome wondering "where they went wrong." Whether having game is a good thing or bad depends solely on the individual. Having game can be good in the sense that it will give you extra boost in the dating game. It can also affect the way you talk and carry yourself. Game is only good if the individual has truthful and good intentions behind it. When you use game to hurt or use somebody for your own personal devious activities, that's when it is considered bad. A person learns the game at various ages; some mostly being as young adults. The experiences we go through teach us what works and what doesn't as well as teaching us what we should do and not do. Game can be taught but trial and error is the form that best works. Not everyone runs game, nor, are they trying to. Some men/women just want someone who is honest with them from the jump and doesn't break their heart. These very few individuals don't have time for the lies and games of others; they will cut someone off instantly if they think someone is playing with them. There is another side of the fence and that side is having the "direct approach." Having this approach means expressing how you feel or expressing your true intentions with total disregard for the consequences. The direct approach can be very effective because it saves time and gets straight to the point. If he/she doesn't get what they want, they usually move on to other prospects in the field. But on the negative side, the direct approach can come off as rude and overly aggressive to some people because it forces pressure on them to either in or go without. Usually, when some give in to this pressure, it's because of sexual attraction or sexual tension that they are feeling while others who may go without simply do because they aren't feeling the person or just not interested like that. The direct approach is most often used by people who display tons of confidence and have a very bold nature. Their tolerance level for games is extremely low and time is everything for an individual that wants to use the direct approach. The goals and objectives of men and women affect game; a person's intention can be either good or bad. Men/women with bad intentions run game with a certain agenda; that agenda could be manipulation or relationship driven or sexual driven. Whenever you have intentions to use and abuse someone those intentions are bad. Having good intentions means looking out for the best interest of each other and it also means being 100% honest. If a person displays honesty and looking out for a person's heart, feelings and interest, they have good intentions. When a woman runs game, she'll use her sex appeal and play to whatever the guys want. This involves telling a guy what he wants to hear which ultimately caters to his ego and pride and leads to the lady getting what she wants in the end. The best way to see if a lady is running game is to take a step back and watch her actions to see if they are genuine and monitor her consistency. One thing you can't do is have sex on the brain so much that you lose focus on who you are dealing with and the type of woman a lady is, in general, because she may implement a three strike rule with your ladies and never be a door mat for any woman. If they fail and strike out, cut her loose because it's better to have a woman who is your source of happiness rather the source of your headaches. Now on the other end, when a man runs game, he directly aims for two places on a woman those places are her mind and her heart. He'll use words of deception to steal her heart and looks and swag to captivate her mind. Once the mind and heart are captured, the legs of a lady get wider and wetter. By the time a woman realizes what happened the damage would have already been done and the guy walks away with another notch on his belt. To counter this, as a woman pays very close attention to a man's actions, make sure he is consistent and don't rush to have sex so fast. Make sure he is your man before he sees you naked and trust your woman's intuition. Know your worth as a woman; don't go giving girlfriend benefits to a man who hasn't earned it.

Game is a part of life and people will try to run it on you in every walk of life. When it comes to game, one key element you have to always pay attention to is actions. Always ask yourself 'does this person actions speak louder than words?', 'are they backing up everything they say that comes out of their mouth or are they just talking?' Always know that time is always on your side and will give you the answers you are looking for. If you have had game ran on you and you came out the situation feeling used, hurt, or played, understand that you can overcome and grow stronger from the situation. Just learning from your mistakes and apply new methods and strategies next time. Game was here before we were born and will be here long after we are gone. The objective isn't to win or lose; it's to value yourself and know your worth and to forever stay striving.

Victim of the Game

You decided to give in to temptation,
You lack patience,
You decided to choose your desire,
Nothing can surpass your fire,
What a shame,
So you decide to run game,
Telling her words of deception,
Effecting her mind & perception,
Your goal is to win,
So you lie & pretend,
Your actions full of sin,
So she finally lets you in,
You smash,
Then you decide to dash,
Your deed is done,
So you think you won,
Sex isn't the only thing you earn,
You soon feel the burn,
You joked & had a good laugh,
Now aids is what you have,
Nobody to blame,
You were victorious & a victim of the game.

. <u>Words of Wisdom</u>

- Ladies you are not an option. You are top priority.

- Fellas, never allow yourself to be a doormat to any woman.

- Fellas, the man makes the clothes; not the other way around.

- Ladies, a real man will treat you as a treasure not like dirt.

- Ladies, never open up your legs to a man you can't trust.

- Stop forcing relationships and work on yourself as an individual.

- Fellas, know when to cut your losses and move on.

- Ladies, never fight over a man.

- The difference between a bad guy and a great man is one will take advantage of you while the other one caters to you.
- Keep a good heart and a great smile and that will forever take you far.

- Best trait for a woman to have is loyalty.

- Best trait for a man to have is ambition.

- Don't rush your relationship. Every relationship travels at its own pace.

- Never settle or be complacent; always strive to the best of your abilities.

Bonus Content

(V.O.S.A)
Volume of Sexual Attraction

Sexual attraction doesn't die; it merely increase and decreases in time.

Sexual attraction can only change with time or working on your appearance

What may be attractive to you at eighteen may be unattractive to you at age twenty-eight; time can change anything.

VOSA can be broken down into four brackets
1. Minor- 0-25%
2. Medium- 26-50%
3. Elevated- 51-75%
4. Exceptional- 76-100%

Minor – means little to no attraction, a complete non-entity, sexual irrelevant.

Medium – friend zone, little attraction, below average, nothing to write home about sexually.

Elevated- above average, good looking, causes sex thoughts, emotions, desires, stimulates curiosity.

Exceptional- causes you to act on it, strong lust, losing focus, strong sexual tension and eager vibe, uncontrollable desire, messed u psyche and causes you to act out of character.

The Hookup Culture

The hookup culture can simply be described as people who accept & engage in casual sexual relationships, one night stands & other activity related in general. The ultimate goal is to focus on pleasure with the emotional connection or long term commitment, many people of all ages engage in "hooking up" bout the vast majority is college students & young adolescents. People who engage in hooking up do so for variety of reasons such instant gratification or to fulfill an emotional need or to pass time & get thru those long winter months known as cuffing season, men are likely to have several hookup partners at once while the women are likely to be happy with just one & usually the most pursued applicant during hooking up with are ex-boyfriends & ex-girlfriends & the reason for this is because there is already an established history between the two parties as well as a sense of comfort zone(especially for ladies). This culture provides a level of fun & adventure for some people in this generation because it has low levels of risk in some areas & of course it's very easy to engage in & there is less risk of rejection plus this new generation prefers the method of "not putting all their eggs in one basket" being open to the possibility anything & everything can potentially have its drawbacks such as emotionally let down, sexually transmitted diseases, sexual abuse as well as other disappointing drawbacks. This hookup culture is putting ideals in the heads of men/women that go against the norm such as the whole ideal of "power lies with the one who cares less" or totally being nonchalant to each other to gain some sort of power or psychological edge in the culture/dating game plus we tend hold our emotions back as humans when it's a very hard thing to do for both sexes. In the culture relationships & feelings are down played & no vulnerabilities can be shown, it seems as if our guard is only down when are clothes are off & our sexual appetite is about to be clinched by someone who catches our eye. Whether you prefer to hookup or not always be open & honest about what your intentions are when it comes to dating because one decision can have a trickle-down effect on many other decisions related to your life, make great & wise choices for your life & especially your health.

10 Steps to Rejuvenation

1. **Self-awareness-** before you conquer any feat you must first know yourself.

2. **Self-evaluation-** what are your flaws and how are you trying to correct them.

3. **Mindset –** how you think of yourself is what you will become.

4. **Yield to action-** action conquers fear; how you approach a problem says a lot about you.

5. **Perseverance-** ability to overcome.

6. **Consistency –** the sign of a champion; anything successful has to be repeated

7. **Leadership-** can you rise to the occasion and lead by example?

8. **Responsibility –** with great power comes responsibility and take control and be held accountable.

9. **Heart-** follow what you feel in your heart because it will act as a guide and your biggest motivation.

10. **Victory & Rejuvenation –** birth of a new you; replenished soul, love and cherish your newfound self and new happiness.

The Friend Zone

- The friend zone is an area where men/women go when there is no attraction.

- The attraction that is non-existent is usually sexual.

- With women, if there is strong sexual attraction, the guy falls into two categories: potential boyfriend or special friend.

- Ladies can be put in the friend zone as well.

- If you are FWB with a person, you are not in the friend zone. You are in a special category of your own.

- Best way to handle the friend zone situation is to avoid getting put in or if you are in to upgrade and change the perception of yourself.

Final Thoughts

The world of dating is forever changing around us. With the evolution of technology and vast variety of relationships, men and women seem to be more at war with each other and at war with themselves. We seem to be growing more careless and we are not expressing our feelings out of fear of getting hurt or played. We put up these guards around our heart so we don't show any vulnerability. This can be our best strength and our biggest downfall if we aren't careful because we escape potential pain and heartbreak but we may be forever alone and may not find love. Life in itself is an adventure leading us from one journey to the next. The one thing you can't be is hesitant because high risk equals high rewards; no matter if it's a goal or a new career or love. You have to not be afraid of what could go wrong emotion or or getting hurt. Just jump in and go for it. The possibilities are endless and each day we are evolving as men and women. Our experiences mold us and shape us daily and yearly. We are learning every day about ourselves as we progress through life. No matter the situation or circumstance, never lose hope and stay striving.

Upcoming Releases

Urban Elements (poetry book)- Fall/Winter 2014

The Sexy Seductive Sagittarius (Erotic Zodiac Novel) – TBA 2014

Transcendence II- Summer 2015

Contact Me

Transcendence page-
www.Facebook.com/transitions101

Email- Bryan88wesley@gmail.com

Twitter -@BryanWesley88

Instagram-Bryan_Wesley88

Website – Under Construction

CPSIA information can be obtained at www.ICGtesting.com
Printed in the USA
BVOW04s2134221214

380503BV00019B/667/P